ISBN: 0-7683-2032-1

Published in 1998 by Cedco® Publishing Company, 100 Pelican Way, San Rafael, CA 94901.
For a free catalog of our entire line of books, write us at the address above
or visit our website: http://www.cedco.com or e-mail us at: sales@cedco.com

Photography Credits

Some photographs have been digitally-manipulated to produce this educational book.
Front cover and back cover photographs © Robert & Linda Mitchell
All interior photos are © Robert & Linda Mitchell, except:
blue damselfly, © Margarette Mead/The Image Bank, and
Malaysian beetle, brown leafhopper, and colorful leafhopper, each © James Carmichael, Jr./The Image Bank

Printed in Hong Kong.

WORLD WILDLIFE FUND

Bugs

honeybee

ladybug

grasshopper

giant leaf-footed bug

tomato hornworm caterpillar

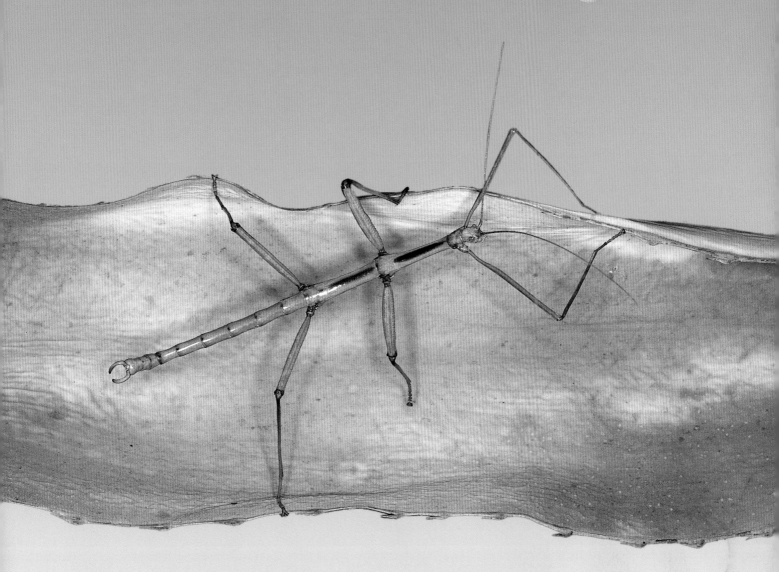

walking stick

orchid mantis

bordered mantis

scarab beetle

ironclad beetle

monarch butterfly caterpillar

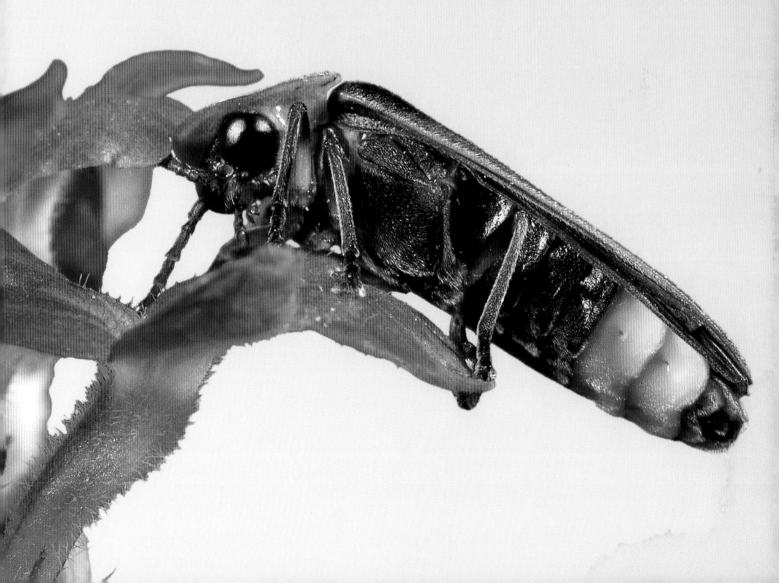

firefly

tailed jay butterfly

indian leaf butterfly

field cricket

black-spot tortoise beetle

red skimmer

blue damselfly

Malaysian beetle

true katydid

green stink bug

large stink bug

brown leafhopper

colorful leafhopper

luna moth